D1414660

with our words,
WE CREATE

Stories Behind the Songs

Jeremy *brotha James* Reisig

.

To my mom, Terri Reisig
Thank you for your dedication to me and
the brotha James mission.
Good catch.

With our words, WE CREATE

FOREWORD

I've known brotha *James* long before even he knew that he would become brotha *James*. For over a decade, from the first time we met in 2001 until 2013, I knew him as Jeremy. We would see each other's names on sales reports, engage in friendly competition, and hang out together on company trips.

However, it wasn't until 2005 that I really got to *know* Jeremy for the inspired and dedicated human being that he is. That was my last year in the Cutco business and I wanted to have my best year ever while leading my colleagues to do the same, so I started a group we called the Ultimate Club. The members of the club were on a mission to each sell $200,000 worth of Cutco. With an average order of a little less than $300 that meant *a lot* of appointments. Over twenty-five sales reps started the year with big dreams of hitting 200K but at the end of the year only Jeremy and I hit the target. It took discipline, motivation and an ability to stay positive even when things didn't go our way.

When I look back on that year, it started with us having a vision for what our future year was going to look like. It required motivation and inspiration to push through the challenging times, especially when we didn't feel like working but picked up the phone and booked appointments anyway. We had to have a strategy on how we were going to reach our goal--a strategy that had a lot to do with the chatter inside of our own heads.

We both stayed positive, we listened to audiobooks and music that inspired us. We knew we had to protect what went into our minds because what came out of our minds was only a reflection of what we let in. We used our words to create the biggest year either of us had ever had at that point in our careers.

After that year I left Cutco to become an author and brotha *James* moved across the country to join a band. Over the years we've both had many adventures. Even though we've been on different paths these last few years, we've stayed in touch and as the Miracle Morning brand grew, so did the brotha *James* brand, leading us to a new type of partnership. I bring brotha *James* to all my live events, including the 400-person *Best Year Ever Blueprint* event in San Diego, CA, and he is also the resident musician in the mastermind group that I co-host with Jon Berghoff, the Quantum Leap Mastermind.

It's been amazing to watch the way people of all ages gravitate to brotha *James'* musical messages and even more amazing to look back on the beliefs we have both used to build our careers. What's exciting is that it's the same basic belief we had when we were two 24-year-olds selling Cutco: **Our input equals our output.** What we allow into our minds is directly connected to the results we are able to produce.

brotha *James'* music has become one of the tools that I use not only for myself, but also to inspire my kids. His music motivates us to live inspired and meaningful lives through the power of words and music. He is a musical messenger who is intentional about each word he puts into his music.

With our Words, WE CREATE: Stories Behind the Songs is a deeper look into the methodical and inspiring mind of brotha *James*. The book is a magnifying glass into his life and into the meaning of the songs he has written over the past four years. This book contains stories of practicing gratitude, acting courageous, being a lover, staying connected to your authentic self, and being an animal in pursuit of your highest hopes and dreams. It is a deep dive into the inspiration for the songs, the lyrics and the lessons brotha James has learned as he creates a brand that is spreading across the world.

Lastly, this book is an opportunity for you to both reflect on your own life and dream of the magnificent future that you deserve. Read, be inspired, and with these words know that you can create anything you desire.

Hal Elrod
Author of the #1 best-selling book,
The Miracle Morning

SPECIAL
INTRODUCTION

Synchronicity

Sitting in solitude on a folding chair, the single piece of furniture in an empty home that our family would soon move into, I looked out of our family room windows into the serenity of the 200-acre Hudson Springs Park. The stillness within the home, something I wasn't used to, would soon make room for sound, as our children--6, 4, and 2--would certainly fill the home with the energetic spirit that only kids know how to do.

What I knew on that day, in November of 2014, was that the circumstances which led to this moment were a reflection of deep introspection, listening to intuition, and acting spontaneously from a place of flow. My wife Mara and I had decided to move, only seven days prior.

We both felt a deep knowing that our lives had slowly drifted away from a connection to our deeper values. We both knew that if we didn't reconsider every aspect of the environment we lived in, the values of the community our children would grow up in, we might wake up one day to a life of regret.

After all, I truly believe the greatest corruption of the soul is when we live with a gap. A gap between those values we claim to hold true, and the way we actually behave. A gap between what we say is important, and the actions we take.

Within twenty-four hours of deciding to move, we put our old home under contract with the eventual buyer. The next day, this home, backing up to deep nature, came on the market. The day after that, we put it under contract to purchase. And the day after that, it was ours.

Some people might believe that spontaneity represents a carelessness or even reckless way of being. This is not in alignment with what I have found to be true. My experience is that there is another kind of spontaneity, one that turns us toward the highest beauty, the greatest good, the most powerful potential of every moment.

This type of spontaneity comes from being so deeply connected to the present that we are able to see the cracks of opportunity life presents to us. My experience has been that the fragile nature of opportunities, often only chance, momentary opportunities, are rarely captured when we live in a waking state of distraction.

Sitting quietly in the chair, my phone rang. This spontaneous phone call was a moment of synchronicity, of which the power could only be discovered many years later.

I answered.

"Hello?"

"Hey, I'm brotha *James*," my new friend said, with a confident equanimity in his voice. "Our mutual friend, Hal, told me to call you."

Unsure that I heard him correctly, I asked, "Can you spell your name for me?"

"Yeah," he calmly replied, "It's b... r... o... t... h... a... James."

"Ah, I get it. Great to meet you, brotha *James*," curious where this would go, as I stared into the trees.

The reason he called was to explore the idea of playing music at an upcoming event for entrepreneurs that I would be hosting with my good friend Hal Elrod. At the time, I really wasn't sure how it would work, or if it was a good idea.

As we got to know each other, as I explored who brotha *James* was and what his music was all about, we began to craft an experiment, a vision for bringing his music into our event of 200+ entrepreneurs, only 30 days away.

We didn't speak again until the event. And I admittedly wasn't really sure how, or why, having his live music was the right thing to do. A very small voice inside of me said this was worth following, worth the risk, worth trying.

Four Years Later

As Steve Jobs famously said, sometimes we can only connect the dots looking backwards. When I look back on that phone call today, I see a chance moment that became a friendship, and a partnership, that has profoundly turned the direction of my life, has changed the future of my family, and has continued to bring transformational, immeasurable value to the communities I lead.

Next week will mark the 40th time brotha *James* and I have teamed up to bring music into a training, community of entrepreneurs, or client event. In the past four years, we have shared the stage for over 7,000 participants who have represented over 75 countries.

From leading my kid's first grade class through music and dream making, to serving as the pillar of inspirational entertainment for our annual Best Year Ever Blueprint event in San Diego, to infusing our LEAF Certification where purpose-driven leaders and entrepreneurs invest north of $10K for a training, the single most complimented aspect of our events is almost always the infusion of brotha *James'* live music.

I remember exactly where I was standing, the sparsely decorated, budget-conscious room set up, the very first time brotha *James* performed the song "Grateful." It was Sunday morning at our inaugural Best Year Ever Blueprint event in December, 2014. Anybody in that room could feel the field of potential, witnessing, participating in a song so transcendent that time itself disappeared. We all saw glimpses of a future that was seeking to emerge in our very presence.

I remember June of 2016, making a smoothie in our kitchen while watching Jeremy play "Animal" with our son Kaizen, two at the time, as Kaizen became one with the music, and then they became one together. Kaizen's love for music, his love for life, has been indelibly shaped by countless jam sessions with brotha *James*, now the Godfather of Kaizen. The greater joy comes from knowing that Kaizen is one of thousands of kids who have been given the gift of brotha *James*, at a time when we need the force of positive messages more than ever.

I remember a 1:00 AM trail run behind our house where Jeremy asked me questions that were way too deep for 1:00 AM. But we dove in anyway. Our time in nature, after many many many trail runs, day and night, has become a time to tune our instrument of friendship, to harmonize our values and behaviors, and to search together for the deeper wisdom in our favorite wind instrument—the woods.

Behind the Music, Behind the Meaning

Within this lifetime of memories, Jeremy has shared his gifts with me and so many others. My highest hope for you, as you explore this book, is that you discover the same gifts that I have. Whether you start with the music, or the messages behind them, consider the lessons we can learn from the man behind it all.

These are some of the qualities that I've observed and learned from my friend brotha *James,* and I hope they can serve as beacons of light, reminders for us all, in how to live life:

Presence--Jeremy brings a presence that invites us all to honor the moment, just a little more deeply. As you enjoy brotha *James* tunes, allow yourself to get lost in the moment; every note, every word, every space between the sound has a reason.

Playfulness--He doesn't just play music, he plays life. He reminds me how fantastic life is when we reclaim the childlike wonder that we were all born with. Remember to let the messages wake up your feet, your hands, your face. Sing, dance, smile, laugh, repeat.

Positivity--The songs speak for themselves. Every moment represents a decision. A decision to guard what goes into our minds and our bodies. A decision to allow the good, the uplifting, the transformative to move through us. brotha *James* made it easy--all you have to do is hit 'play'.

Purposeful--I know few people who have a stronger internal compass than brotha *James*. If your life is a constant creation of a song, what rhythm are you creating? Who are you making music with? What notes are you putting into your body--from the conversations you have to the food you eat? What mission is your music serving? Will others want to keep listening even when you aren't around?

Thank you, Jer, for giving me the gifts of your influence, your art, your mission. Thank you to each of you reading this book, singing brotha *James* tunes, as we are one tribe. We are all in this world together, co-creating a future that we all hope is flourishing.

Jon Berghoff
President, Flourishing Leadership Institute

INTRODUCTION

Dear Friend,

We can use the power of music as a tool in our lives. When we listen to uplifting, meaningful and inspirational music, it can lift our spirits. It can give us a burst of energy, and it can help us to have the extra ounce of courage we need to make a breakthrough in some area of our lives. The music I have created is my vision for positively impacting the world. I write songs about being courageous, loving selflessly, developing self-awareness, and remaining optimistic. I have worked hard to create music that you will love.

If you're a music lover like me, you have listened to thousands of songs in your lifetime. I still remember the first band I really got into when I was ten years old--Pearl Jam and the album was *Ten*. Wow, did I fall in love with that band. I listened to their album non-stop while I rode the bus to school, walked the family dogs after dinner, and sat in the back seat of the car on family trips. Pearl Jam was my band of the 90s!

Do you have a favorite band or artist? I know sometimes it can be hard to narrow it down to just one. So think of all your favorite bands and songs. Now consider the messages and the meanings behind those favorite songs. What are the stories? Do the messages align with your values? Do they empower you? Or do they disempower you?

Most of us are affected by the music and words we listen to most often; whether their impact is big or small, music and words possess power. However, many times we do not stop to think about what effect the songs we listen to might have on us. We drive down the road singing the hit breakup song on the radio at the top of our lungs and then wonder why we are dissatisfied with our mate. Or we listen to a song with offensive language and wonder why we slip with our words.

Have you ever heard the phrase that our input equals our output? The words we hear often help to create our internal vocabulary, and that internal vocabulary shapes how we talk about our world. The lens through which we see the world then plays a role in the way we interact with it. When I say interact I mean the way we respond to the uncertainty that is the world: the highs, the lows, the celebrations, the failures. The music we listen to and the messages in the music can play a big part in this engagement for better or worse.

Granted, an abundance of music features lyrics about hard partying, violence, and meaningless relationships; these songs are definitely in the mix of music I have listened to from time to time. I remember blasting some Master P when I was seventeen years old. The sounds, the beats, the overall feel just drew me in. However, there is also the music that inspires me to be a better boyfriend, musician, and overall human being. I notice when I sing or play these tunes I am affirming to myself the person I want to be and it feels good, not just in the moment, but also in the way I interact with my brother, parents, girlfriend, and community. Noticing this difference in how music makes me feel has not only changed the way I listen to music, but inspired the way I make music. It has deepened my purpose to write music that helps us to be the best version of ourselves.

This book is comprised of the stories about what inspired the lyrics in the songs, and the journey the songs took to get to the version which you hear today. For the sake of organizing the book, I have placed the stories in the order of conception of the song. Some songs moved from conception to production in less than a year; however, many took years to find their final form.

Let me also explain some of the terminology I use in the stories. For example, I refer to myself as being a looper. Looping is the process of using technology to layer sounds over the top of one another to create a full band effect as a solo artist. I personally loop guitar, keyboards, vocals and drum sounds. It is an incredible technology. (To get a visual of this, google brotha *James*, "Animal," NPR Tiny Desk.)

Something else I would like to clarify is the way I refer to my lyrics. I use terms like chorus, pre-chorus, verse, and bridge. Let me quickly explain by starting with the chorus, the main point or idea in the song. It is almost always repeated multiple times. Another component of the song is the pre-chorus which generally precedes the chorus and consists of two to four repeated lines that lead the listener into the chorus. Next, the verse, usually at the beginning of the song, sets up a story that relates to the idea in the chorus. Typically, two verses appear in my songs. Finally, the bridge generally comes after the second chorus and is sometimes a continuation of the theme (or it might take you in a completely different direction) before it bleeds back into the chorus for one more dose of the familiar melody and words. My songs usually end with a double chorus.

And one more clarification. The journal questions at the end of each story are added for one reason. I believe that the questions we consistently ask ourselves determine the quality of our lives. The better the questions we ask, the better the answers we receive. It does not matter who you are or where you are from, if you take the time to ask and answer these questions you will gain new insights on how amazing you are. (Answering them in a journal is best so you have a record of your thinking.)

My highest hope for both the CD and book is that they inspire you to live a meaningful life on which you can look back and be proud.

Please enjoy.

Love,
brotha *James*

EVOLVE

The writing was on the wall. Funktion, the seven-piece funk rock band I had been a percussionist and rapper with for four years, was coming to an end. Inside of me a voice kept screaming: "YOU ARE A MUSICIAN!" I had no choice other than to go solo. But I had a problem.

When Funktion ended in 2013, I could not sing a song without hitting dozens of wrong notes. I could not play a full tune on guitar without playing a wrong chord, and I had zero experience being a looper. But that did not stop me. I was determined to be a musician traveling the world, inspiring people to live inspired lives. I remember sitting down at my office desk and writing the lyrics to "Evolve." In the first verse I sing

As I write this rhyme
I begin to see the sign
This is a story to myself

A message to remind
Me of who I'm meant to be
Planted like a little seed
I'm growing like an oak tree
Where the roots are running deep.

The words poured out of me so naturally. I put the pen to paper and the lyrics wrote themselves. This song has been a staple in my sets for the last four years and always reminds me of the person I want to be. These words are a constant reminder to follow my passions, to remember that I am on the right track, and to know it is a slow journey but so worth it!

I feel as if my journey is one that was always meant to be. This song is about using the journey to be the best version of myself. In the chorus I remind myself that

The time has come
No longer judge
Spread the love to one another
Be as one
Have some fun
Support your sisters and your brothers.

Well, in this spin
Look within
Ask yourself what can be given
Time, energy, your money
The more you give the more you're living.

I desire to be a person who is compassionate, who takes the time to help other people feel good by giving to others with my time, my energy, and my money. Each of us has a different way of giving something of ourselves to the world. As I get older, I realize I am judgmental sometimes, to the point where before I even know a person I am profiling him or her. I create expectations based on the stories I am telling myself about the person. These chorus lyrics help to program myself to be less judgmental and to be the change I wish to see in the world. The time to evolve is not tomorrow or a year from now, but right now.

We are all constantly evolving as individuals and as a species. The second verse talks about learning from our struggles and our mistakes in order to grow into the person we are meant to be.

And I know we go through things that can be frustrating
If you really pay attention you can see them demonstrating
How to grow up
How to EVOLVE
How to take the past mistakes
Apply to present problems and solve.

With this I've been changing my gaze
And letting in rays
Taking a hard look at me and changing my ways
No longer wanna live my life a fighting the haze
I say goodbye to my addictions and vibrations are raised.

This is the first song I released as brotha *James*. Even today I love singing it. "Evolve" is an affirmation to pay attention to the direction I am headed in, to choose the attitude I have, to consider the habits I adopt, and that, at the end of the day, to realize I am not perfect and can learn from my mistakes.

My highest hope is that the song helps you reflect on the times in your lives where you have learned lessons, become less judgmental, or acted to evolve into the person you want to become.

To download a free copy of the song, please go to this URL:
brothajames.com/evolve

～～～ Journal Questions ～～～

As you look back on your life, remember a time when you evolved in some way. This could be a time when you grew physically, emotionally, relationally, or spiritually. When you reflect on that time, think about the new perspectives you gained or lessons you learned.

How will the perspectives you gained from that experience or experiences help you evolve in the days, weeks, and years to come?

How will they help you become the person you are meant be?

DREAMER

In 2013, I was in a relationship with Kelly. She and I had been together for a couple of years and experienced some amazing adventures, including touring with the Funktion guys around the country for 175 shows in one year. During those tours we had some epic battles! This song describes my belief that a loving relationship could happen even though we had gone through challenges. It is about believing that love is worth working for, even fighting for. The chorus says,

I'm a dreamer
A believer
In love I know it's true.
I know that I can work it out and give my love to you.
I might fall down but I'll get up if you would love me too
Let's dream of a life together and make it all come true.

I know I am going to screw up because I am not perfect. I know we are going to have challenges, but I want to work through them. I want us to dream of a life where we are both excited for the future. It cannot all be what I am excited about—we have to dream it up together.

Back then I would frequently go to a Better Health Store to buy healthy food. One day I pulled into the parking lot and had the urge to write down lyrics to "Dreamer." I popped open my Notes App on my iPhone and wrote the chorus.

After writing it, I started to think about what Kelly and I had been through. That is where the verse idea came from. When she and I first met, we were both coming out of broken relationships; we were both a little sad. The first verse reflects that pain:

You and me are looking for something
To get away from the pain in our hearts.

In contrast, the second verse is about the future:

I wanna run around the world, just a boy and a girl
Living the good life
I wanna hold your hand and be your man I wanna
Do this love right.

My selfishness had to be dismantled and put aside if I was going to show up fully in the relationship. I needed to work at being a better boyfriend for her than I had been for anyone else. I wanted to lift her up, encourage her, have her encourage me, and go forward together as a happy couple in future adventures together.

The bridge explains this:

I'm just a boy and you're just a girl
We're just another set of lovers
Running through this world.

Relationships can be tough and they take work. This will be a common theme that is evident in the other love songs I have written. More and more I am realizing that relationships are tough, even a little crazy. Lots of couples are trying to figure out how to make it work. We were not any different.

My highest hope for this song is that it inspires you to take a look at your relationships and to celebrate them.

To download a free copy of the song, please go to this URL:
brothajames.com/dreamer

Journal Questions

Think of the times in your life when you have been there to encourage, lift up or just listen to your current partner, or, if you are single, consider a partner you have had in the past. In what ways were you there for him or her? In what ways did he or she show up for you?

What aligned goals are you and your partner working toward? This could be quality family time, financial goals or something as simple as some scheduled date nights.

And if you are not currently in a relationship, what qualities are you looking for in a partner?

REUNITE

This was a beast of a song to write. I remember having so many lyric ideas for this one. I was at a Tony Robbins event called *Date with Destiny* with my bestie Brad Weimert. It was an intense event and we needed our sleep. But right as we were falling asleep, I felt the urge to write lyrics so I went into the bathroom, sat in the bathtub and wrote this:

You been living in me for years
You be giving me the strength to fight my fears
Helping me to break through the smoke and mirrors
Humbling me to shed my tears.

The song is about the little kid that lives inside each of us. YOU know, the one that has all the answers because he or she is connected to the source of what we really are.

In these lyrics, I am talking to that little guy inside of me--the kid who has been in there since the beginning of my life. Before I was influenced by society, I remember being very clear on my passions: I wanted to be a Chicago Cubs baseball player or a musician. Particularly drawn to being a drummer or a singer, I would get my family together and make them listen to me hit on pots and pans, while I performed 4 Non Blondes. I still remember the excitement in my heart during these moments. Even though it was over thirty years ago, these moments seem like they happened yesterday. As I grew up, I gradually lost track of that voice inside me and became obsessed with material wealth. I coveted a cool sports car, a big screen TV, elaborate sound systems, and big black leather couches. However, the more I purchased and showed off, the emptier I felt.

This track reminds me to reunite with that childlike innocence that just wanted to play baseball and music. As I got into my early thirties (I'm now thirty-seven), I started to empower the little kid again. I started to say yes to what I was passionate about and that is where the chorus came from.

The chorus reminds me

> **This is our time to shine**
> **It's time to reunite**
> **I know that we will find**
> **We're gonna find a way to carry on.**

The beginning of this song acknowledges the voice of little brotha *James* getting louder and louder, and how I finally began to surrender to this voice. In these lyrics from the first verse, I literally talk to myself:

I can hear you coming
Are you a friend of mine
I'd like to welcome you to my town right now
You're here to teach me something about this simple life
Together we're gonna turn the world upside down.

The bridge reflects what I have learned in my life's journey when I pulled away from my passions. Even though I seemed to be pulled off track, I still gained new tools: business, communication, and organizational skills. The bridge also combines learning these skills with remembering who it is I am meant to be:

My ages on these pages
These pages are leaving traces
These traces are guiding the mazes
And they're the mazes of my life.

You burning like dynamite
You're living deep inside
With you right by my side
I'm ready for this fight.

When we reunite with the childlike wonder and playfulness that lives inside each of us, we unleash a new superpower which helps us connect to deeper meaning and fulfillment.

My highest hope for you is that this song and story inspire you to investigate your own childlike voice--the one that has been subtly there below the surface, whispering in your ear. I hope you are able to use it as a guide in your life; if you have kids, I want you to be able to help them stay more closely connected to their authentic selves.

To download a free copy of the song, please go to this URL:
brothajames.com/reunite

～～ Journal Questions ～～

When you were a little boy or girl, what did you love to do?

Before anyone started to tell you what to do, what were you naturally attracted to?

How might you reunite with that childlike part of yourself? This could be a game you could play, a song you could listen to, or an old friend you could reconnect with. What about taking a lesson of some kind, or joining a league?

How might reuniting with this interest spark an energy inside you that would spill over into other areas of your life?

Have fun with this!

GRATEFUL

I n college and just twenty years old, I was lucky to have been recruited into Vector/Cutco, a marketing company with a heavy emphasis on personal growth. Through one of their summer conferences, I was exposed to the idea of gratitude.

At the time I was pretty resistant to any sort of personal growth and what it entails. At the age of twenty-two, however, I started to listen to self-motivational CDs and cassettes. (I know--when was the last time you listened to a cassette tape?) As a result, I became aware of the idea that one's income and fulfillment will rarely exceed one's level of personal growth. I knew I wanted to grow my physical, emotional, intellectual, and spiritual life, but what is the point in having an amazing family, making tons of money, and possessing savings, cars, homes, etc., if I never felt grateful for the life I live?

The lyrics in the first verse reflect the start of my actual gratitude journey:

There came a time in my life
When I knew I had to try
And open up my eyes
It seemed so simple to me
Why such a struggle to be
My own insecurities
Creeping up on me.

Practicing gratitude is similar to eating healthy; we know it is good for us yet we still resist doing so. The song becomes a musical affirmation reminding me to think about what I am grateful for each time I hear the track.

When I was thirty, I read a book called *The Magic of Thinking Big* by Dr. David Schwartz. In the book, Schwartz asks readers to do a gratitude exercise, for example, enumerating the people, places, or opportunities they are thankful for. Right then I started to practice gratitude and have ever since. I started writing a few comments every night about what I was grateful for and that soon turned into five to ten comments before I went to bed. Now I go to bed and wake up feeling deeply appreciative for the life I get to live. The practice of gratitude, especially on the most challenging of days, brings me to a place of appreciation for the people in my life, my environment, and for the opportunities that lie ahead. This practice also allows me to appreciate myself because each day I write something about myself for which I feel gratitude.

In the introduction of this book, I talked about the important role that questions play in our lives. The practice of gratitude starts with one simple question and I present this question as the chorus of this song:

What am I grateful for?
I think about the little things
What am I grateful for?
So many simple things.

When we ask *What am I grateful for*, instantly our brains start to formulate answers. When we take the time to write these answers down, we become more closely connected to what is already great in our lives--family, pets, sunsets, clean water, good health, shelter, an optimistic view of the world. The list is endless.

Before I ask you to think about what you are grateful for, I want to tell you a quick story about the second verse. My friend Kosha Dillz is an amazing rapper who lives in Los Angeles. During the production of this song, he stopped by the studio and laid down this verse:

Woke up with a stretch and a yawn
So darn tired gotta mow this lawn
Gotta call my mom, go to the studio
A couple hours out gotta write this song
Could be worse if I was fighting a war
Dying from a disease with no real cure
Homeless on the streets so cold and poor
And I'm here complaining about all these chores
What am I so grateful for, I gotta write it down
So that it makes some sense
About having a job, paying some rent
Food on the table, respect for all my ladies and gents
Speaking in languages, taking it in

Surfing waves in the sunshine and catching a tan
Clean clothes on my back and a couple of raps
My family and kit kats how about that.

The best part is he wrote this verse in one hour! Kosha reminds me to be grateful for the little things that are so easy to take for granted.

This track has reached way beyond what I ever imagined, bringing families and friends together all over the world. It will continue to be my mantra as I move through life's adventures. My highest hope for this song is that you are inspired to think about all you have to be grateful for in your life.

To download this song for free,
please text Grateful to the number 44222

Journal Questions

What are you grateful for right now?

Who are you grateful for?

What about yourself are you grateful for?

Who could you write, call, or text to offer gratitude?

ANIMAL

I often think about the day I am going to die. When that day comes, I want to look back and know I gave life all I had: I went after my passions, and I am proud of myself. I want to look back and see that I lived life BIG! That is what I was thinking when I wrote the chorus to this song:

I'm an animal
I want my belly full
I will not go to my grave
With this inside of me.

I'm an animal
And I can feel the pull
It's time to open my cage
And see who I can be.

I remember so clearly the moment this chorus came to life. I was living in Austin, Texas, and was in the middle of a jam session, with the chorus loop playing over and over. I was asking myself what I should say here and just as quickly as I asked that question the words appeared. I started to jump up and down screaming, "I'm an animal, I want my belly full!" I loved singing those words. As I wrote them down and finished the remainder of the chorus, I realized this song was for *me*.

In the process of becoming brotha *James*, I needed inspiration to become a musician. At the time, I had not played any shows. All I had done was practice in my apartment. This track was a big inspiration for me to keep working through the challenges that come when we journey toward our dreams. I am reminding myself to push through those challenges and turn my dreams into reality.

I also realized that many of the obstacles we need to break through in order to create the life of our dreams are internal. The second verse of the song speaks to that concept:

> **Escape, now create my own state**
> **I'm the one with the power**
> **Dictate my own fate**
> **Persist to exist**
> **Now make a list**
> **Of the egos in my life I must dismiss.**
>
> **Battle in the mind**
> **To know that I'm divine**
> **That I'm the mastermind**
> **In this day-to-day grind.**

Some things in life we can control but others we cannot. This second verse is about what we can control--the ability to be self-aware, the decision to empower our minds with good fuel, and the power to remember that we are often better than we give ourselves credit for being.

The first verse is one of my favorites to sing because it reminds me of the journey that I am on and that I am willing to do what it takes to turn my visions for an amazing future into reality:

I feel it burning, deep in my soul
I know it's time for me to go
In this journey, I take it slow
Assess my prey before I start to hone.

I am talking about the ability to connect to that deep burning for the person I am meant to be in my life. At the same time, I have used intelligence in my brotha *James* journey; I have been patient and calculated. Each time I sing this verse, it reminds me I can envision the journey ahead and see the person I need to become in order to succeed.

I want to finish this chapter by talking about the bridge of the song; it is about people coming together to leave clues to help future generations step into their full human potential. These clues can help them bypass the struggles we have had to endure in our own lives and as a species. The bridge lyrics call for this action:

I know who it is we be
Let's change this world we see

Leaving these crumbs and seeds
It's time to bare our teeth.

I'm a lion, you're a lion
I wanna hear you roar
Well, I'm a lion, you're a lion
It's time for you and me to ROAR!

My highest hope for this song is that you are able to go after your dreams with an animalistic pursuit. Most animals tap into an innate sense of purpose that helps them push through when all the odds are stacked against them. That is what I want for all of us.

*To download this song for free,
please text Animal to the number 33444*

~~~ Journal Questions ~~~

Think about your journey. Reflect on a time when you went after something important to you--a passion, a relationship, a career, for example. What inspired you to be animalistic in the pursuit of your goal?

When you imagine the next one to three years of your life, what excites you the most? What are you looking forward to?

MY LIFE

riting these stories has reminded me of the progression I have made as a musician. I had never actually been a singer before 2013, so I realized I needed to take vocal lessons. I could feel music inside of me, but I had to figure out a way to get it to the world. It has been an incredibly long road to be the singer I am today.

In the first verse I sing these words:

Born with the music in my mind
I write songs that give me life
Thirty-seven years what a beautiful ride
The more I seek the more I find.

Taking vocal lessons made me understand that if I could learn to sing at thirty-three, then I should be able to learn anything. I tapped into one of the great gifts of being human. That gift is to make lots of small decisions that lead to big results and ultimately to transformation. We all have the power to choose; we simply have to prepare ourselves to make the tough choices in those challenging moments.

This song is about overcoming the challenges we face to take ownership of our lives. It is about being the authentic *you* and encouraging others to do the same. For me, I have to let go of the voice inside my head which is always chatting about doubt. I hear that voice almost every day. Sometimes it is yelling in my ear; other times it is an annoying whisper I can just barely hear. This song reminds me to stay strong, to ask quality questions, and to believe in myself.

When I started writing this track, I considered the world we live in. I pondered the influence of entertainment, social media, corruption, politics, and even our own self-judgment. I thought about how even though these forces try to control us, we still have the ability to make our own way if we are strategic in our thinking. If we focus our attention in the right areas of our lives, we are able to overcome the grips of society and our own internal demons. When we focus on what is going right and what is already working, we tap into positivity and energy that help us create a fulfilling life.

These ideas are reflected in the first verse:

How to navigate the mainstream
With positivity
Live, love, grow, it's a human capability
See all the good things
And give 'em energy
Here I go, it's time to spread my wings.

This first verse then sets up the chorus:

This is my life
I know I can be
Anything I wanna dream
Focus like a laser beam.

This is my life
I know I can be
Living like a free bird,
I'm gonna give it everything.

These lyrics affirm that I can make my dreams come true if I focus on those dreams and give them everything. The line "Living like a free bird" is a tribute to the birds I see flying effortlessly through the sky; it is a reminder to let the universe allow opportunities, people, and experiences to flow into my life.

This song has been turned upside down from its first version, but on this album it has found a home. Even through all of this song's versions, there remains a consistent theme: the deep belief that I can conceive, believe, and achieve my dreams. Some of the strategies I have used to make dreams come true are being grateful, being passionate about what my dreams are, and lifting others up.

The second verse takes this into account:

When I look up into the sky
I say I'm grateful for my life
Soften up to who's inside
The more I sing the more I'm gonna find.

How to move with the movement
A key ingredient
Consent to what we love
And then we'll find a new intelligence.

My time spent
Throwing positive
Vibrations to who it is
That's gonna need it next.

If we get to our goals and dreams without helping others do the same, I believe we will find the end result less fulfilling. For me, that means spreading positive energy everywhere I go. I want to be the spark in the room which generates belief in others and in the collective consciousness of the group. This is what the song represents.

My highest hope for this song is that it gives you the ability to believe in yourself. That you can sing the words and feel empowered to go out into the world--creating the life of your dreams while, at the same time, lifting up other people.

To download this song for free,
please text Mylife to the number 44222

 Journal Questions

When have you been inspired to go after a dream of your own?

When is a time that you felt inspired by someone else going after his or her dream?

When you look into the future, what are one or two dreams you have?

LOVIN'

This song started as a breakup song. Not an ordinary breakup song though. It was a gentle, connected and respectful song about being open and honest in a relationship.

When I wrote "Lovin'" (initially titled "Wonder"), I was trying to let go of a relationship and to make some sense of it. For a couple years I was really proud of the song. Playing it over and over these last few years, however, I have recognized that I was not as proud of myself as I once thought I was. Because I was selfish and unable to really be there for my girlfriend, I didn't show up in the relationship to allow it to last. This song is about making the shift and putting love as a priority, not just in my schedule but in my mind.

While writing this song, I entered into a meaningful relationship. Since I have been determined to grow as a partner in the relationship, I have felt a stronger and stronger pull to make the song reflect staying together, not breaking up. And when I started reading

Regi Campbell's book *What Radical Husbands Do*, I knew the song had to go in a *stay together, make it work, choose love* direction.

The chorus is now about appreciating the other person in the relationship and programming myself to fall into a deeper state of love with my partner.

I know about me, I know about you
Lovin' has made it through
I wanna thank you for the truth my friend
Now I can see
You and me
We were meant to be
We're gonna help each other dream till the end
Fallin' in lovin'
Lovin' you
Fallin' in lovin'
Lovin' you.

As we all know, relationships are tricky and enough triggers convince us that our relationships might not work. Well, I am here to say try harder! That is what the song is about--supporting each other's dreams but also having a shared dream. It is about strong and honest communication. It is about being more selfless than you have ever been. It is not easy, but from what I can tell, it is worth it, both for the way you feel and the way you make your partner feel. This song is about being in love.

Lyrically, I mix my rap style cultivated during my years in Funktion with my ever-growing ability to sing. Both verses are rap and contrast with the pre-chorus and chorus which are more melodic. The rap in the first verse is the story of meeting each other for the first time; it relates the incredible power of love in the beginning and then the struggles that come a little later down the road.

Verse one explains the beginning:

We started off with some hot and heavy love
You're cooler than I'd ever dreamed of
So quickly clicking, like we were meant to be
I was made for you and you were made for me.

Circumstances made it easy to do
Now we're moving in together under one roof
No calculations on what we're going to do
Two young lovers with nothing to lose.

This situation had some disagreements coming
Now we both got emotions that are running
It's such a battle to fight with one you love
It's getting rough.

I structured the lyrics to remind myself that even in times of struggle we can come together in our relationships and find love. Maybe you had a relationship that is no longer; if you are singing along to this song consider the lines in the chorus that say "We were meant to be." I ask what you learned from that relationship to help you in your next relationship. *Meant to be* does not mean it is going to last forever; it simply means that at that moment in your journey something special emerged. From being together, each of you may have learned to be more aware and able as a partner.

What sticks with me about this song is the power of our minds to create a wonderful relationship. The thoughts we allow ourselves to think, the stories we tell ourselves, can be destructive to the relationship. When I initially wrote this song, I was not a great boyfriend; in fact, I was a terrible boyfriend. Much of that was because I focused on what was wrong, broken and missing, versus what was right, working and wonderful. I like to think of this song as a reminder of being in love: the journey, the challenges, and the ability to focus on what is working instead of what is not.

The pre-chorus of this song

We got fears and we're pushing through
Through the years I'll be lovin' you

reminds us how lucky we are someone is willing to be our partner in our life's journey. I hope this song helps us all to try harder in our relationships, to remember to use our mental energy to create positive thoughts about our partners. And, to be more curious about how to be a great and giving partner ourselves.

To download a free copy of the song, please go to this URL:
brothajames.com/lovin

Journal Questions

When have you chosen lovin' instead of judgin'? (Guys, this might be a time when we just listened and did not try fixin'.)

When is a time you overcame a fear in a relationship in order to give the relationship a chance to thrive?

How can you be a great partner in your current relationship?

FEELIN' IT

This song is about getting out of my comfort zone and taking action toward my dreams. When I first started the brotha *James* project, I had to go with the gut feeling that I was made for this journey. I did not know exactly how it was all going to work out but I had to act anyway. In the song's first verse, I reference feeling the pull, being a little reserved, but taking the chance anyway:

> **Sometimes I'm sitting in the back of the room**
> **I know exactly what it is I wanna do**
> **I wanna get up, dance, romance**
> **Get the ants out of my pants**
> **It's time to make my move**
> **It's time to take a chance.**

As I have mentioned in previous chapters, I had no idea what this adventure would entail, so I had reservations and those reservations were (and sometimes are still) "the ants in my pants."

Going after my dream is romantic. When I am giving into the passion of making music, the connection I have with both the creative process and the final product moves through me. I possess a deep love for making uplifting and inspirational music; I feel a sense of fulfillment when I am in that state of flow whether at a live show or in the basement of my house with my guitar.

The second verse is a tribute to the positive effects of being involved with Tony Robbins' ideas. It is an affirmation to myself, a reminder to take deep breaths so I can clear my mind. Singing this part of the song reminds me of how important it is to breathe! (The 1-4-2 is a breathing technique where I breathe in for 4 counts, hold for 16 counts, and then let out for 8 counts.)

1- 4- 2--Say yes and make my move
It's time to take the steps that gonna help me find my groove
Wanna be the seed, believe
There is no they, just you and me
Mix my authenticity
With what I think the world might need.

This verse is also about the journey I am on to find the avenues through which I can align my talents and strengths with what the world is asking for. We are all given unique skills and capabilities to help us both survive and thrive as individuals and as a species.

The pre-chorus is a countdown to take some action. Every time I sing it I think of going after my dreams and goals and turning them into reality!

1 2 3 4--Get my body on the floor
5 6 7 8--It's time to celebrate.

The celebrate line is a trigger for me to be proud of myself--to jump up and down with enthusiasm as I have both small and big wins on the path to making this an incredible life adventure. It is also a reminder to help other people celebrate when they have a win or breakthrough in their lives.

The chorus of this track is so simple:

Feelin' it, I'm feelin' it.

It is about being in the flow of life, about being connected to the alignment of talent, strength, enjoyment, impact, and opportunity. It is that place in life where we are locked into our bliss. In its simplicity, the chorus is a great reminder there is no need to make things complicated.

Simple but powerful, the horn lines and lyrics fit together. My producer Carlos Sosa is such an incredible talent that I am humbled to work with him. He pushes me to grow and is a key partner in making this music come alive.

My highest hope for this song is that it inspires you to ask how can your unique talents and strengths align to make the world a better place. So often, the world can overwhelm us and drive us to live in a safe place: a job we do not really like but it pays the bills; a relationship that is not our ideal relationship and a disconnect from what truly makes us come alive. This song was created to help us connect to the power living inside each of us to experience our potential.

To download this song for free,
please text Feelinit to the number 33444

Journal Questions

What do you believe are your greatest talents and strengths? When you think about this question you might find that you are courageous, persistent, compassionate, determined, a good listener, a great athlete, a great teacher or coach.

How might you use your talents to add value to your family, community and the world?

PLEASE STOP

A break up with a girlfriend was unfortunately still on my mind, even though it had been years since we separated. I would remember the discomfort I felt when we were together. I can still connect to the uncertainty I was feeling 24/7 and am often reminded of the lesson I learned. I was weak in my ability to stand up for myself; I was a wimp.

The lyrics of the bridge

I walk up to your room
I'm ready to tell you
That it's time for me to be walking away
You're asking me to stay
My heart it gets afraid
And I walk away

portray almost exactly how the breakup happened. I actually walked up the stairs up to her room and asked her to never text me and to please stop calling. That's where the title for the song came from. I can so vividly remember almost everything about that day. My hands were shaking, my heart was racing, and I was about to cry.

The song is about the decision to move on from a toxic relationship. Late nights, drugs, parties and poor rituals--all contributed to me feeling more unhappy than ever before in my life. But at the same time, it was addicting to feel that way. I could see the writing on the wall though. I knew inside I wanted to be more, give more, do more. I knew it was up to *me* to make the tough decision to end that particular relationship. If I couldn't, then who was going to make it for me?

When I ended the relationship, I said what I say in the chorus:

Please stop calling
I'm done talking
Don't come crawling back to me.

I'm done stalling
No more falling in love.

I was not really in love with her; I was infatuated and just wanted her to like me. Something about the way she made me chase her was addicting. I talk about this in the first verse of the song:

Sink your teeth in
Let it begin
Now you're livin' within

> **Inside of my mind**
> **I try to deny it**
> **That you are poison.**

I was defenseless against the game she was playing with me. I was rundown, tired, and emotionally drained all the time. I never knew how she was going to wake up in the morning. Would she be happy, angry, depressed, anxious, or everything in-between? I never knew, so I was always on high alert and anxious.

In the first half of the second pre-chorus, I reference the constant battle in my mind:

> **Can't stop thinking about you**
> **All that you ever do**
> **Is make me feel like I'm crazy and**
> **I'm losing my mind.**

She had a superpower to make me feel I was lost. She made me believe I was doing everything wrong and was not what she wanted. Have you ever had someone make you feel that way? It is painful.

The first pre-chorus and the second half of the second pre-chorus both say,

> **Gotta stop thinking about you**
> **I know what I got to do**
> **I got to say goodbye.**

Have you ever known exactly what you need to do, yet you are so stuck in your head that you feel paralyzed? That is the way I felt. I am so grateful that I walked up to that room and broke it off.

My life will forever be changed by that decision. Never will I be in a relationship like that again. Ultimately, I am inspired, appreciative, and empowered from having suffered through that painful experience. Seven years later, I am still proud of myself, and return to that strength when faced with turmoil.

Recently, I have recognized a parallel to my relationship with that woman and relationships that currently exist in different parts of my life, for example, with caffeine or alcohol or sugar. It is as if they become the very thing to which I need to say "Please Stop." (Note: When I ended the relationship I actually said, "**Please** stop calling: Don't call, don't text, I'm done." I am a polite man, even in the heat of the moment. Authentic, well-used manners are a superpower.)

I have learned that we must be aware of what is lifting us up and what is bringing us down. My hope is that the song helps you, my listeners, to be strong and capable of standing up for the person you are now, and for the person you want to be in the future.

To download a free copy of the song, please go to this URL:
brothajames.com/pleasestop

～～～ Journal Questions ～～～

When is a time in your life that you said please stop to a challenging relationship with a person or an addictive substance or activity? Take a minute to reflect on the experience or experiences and think about the lessons you learned.

How will those lessons make you stronger for the future?

SLOW DOWN

It's time to slow down
And give myself a little love right now.

I was having an impromptu jam session in the driver's seat of my Honda Odyssey tour van. The beautiful fresh water of Grand Traverse Bay was right in front of me. I started to sing "It's time to slow down, and give myself a little love right now." I got out of my van and started to cry. It hit me that each day I struggle to appreciate the moment. The song is a trigger for me to slow down--physically and mentally--and fill myself with love and appreciation. Too often I have moved so quickly that I do not take the time to step back and gain perspective.

In the first verse, I introduce the idea of how our world creates pressures on us:

Since I was young, I've been moving fast
Trying to be cool, keep up with the rest

Trophies, popularity and being the best dressed
I even did some hurtful things, just to progress.

I must confess that I was confused
Young kid living in a small town just trying to be cool
Losing myself, losing my truth
I don't know what it was I was trying to prove.

This verse sums up my childhood. I wanted to wear what the cool kids wore; I wanted to be in the popular group; and I wanted to be the one who was the best on the athletic field. I was always trying to be a cool kid so I did what the cool kids did. Joining in when they made fun of someone, I molded myself to act the way I thought they would need me to be in order to be accepted.

I am from a small town where everyone knows everyone else, and I wanted everyone to know and like me. Still, I have a strong desire to be someone for other people. My friend Hal Elrod has an awesome quote that I've found really helpful over the past several years. He says, "Trade in being perfect for being authentic." I love this quote because it reminds me not to try so hard to be someone I am not. My real value to the world is to be the best version of myself that I can be, not the best version of what I think other people want me to be.

This song is about acknowledging and connecting to the strength that lives inside each one of us. *Slow down* means take the time to acknowledge and appreciate the talents, strengths and unique capabilities that we each possess. I recently started taking the time to look in the mirror at myself and say things like *I love you* or *I'm proud of you.*

Slowing down is in many ways the subtle art of speeding up. For me, this has been a big breakthrough in the way I see my past, present, and future. I slow down and see them all working in partnership to provide information, intelligence, and inspiration to help me move through the daily adventure of being human.

In the bridge, I explain why slowing down matters:

Slow down
I'm moving too fast, I'm out of control
Slow down
I'm gonna figure out which way I'm heading
Slow down
It's time for me to connect to my soul
Fill it up so I can send it out.

Slowing down not only gives us time to appreciate but also allows time to plan how to create more magic in our lives. I have heard it said that if we fail to plan, we plan to fail. That has been so true in my life. I am grateful every day for this song and the way it forces me to be present in the moment.

On the most basic level, I discover a deep sense of gratitude when I take time to remind myself that I am alive. I do not know about you, but I have seen friends, family members, and strangers face some serious challenges. Some of them have even faced death and here I am worried whether I am going to sing a note perfectly. Slowing down is the key ingredient for me to feel fulfilled and appreciative in the present moment.

My highest hope for this song is that it inspires people to be present and enjoy the beauty in their lives--family, friends, relationships, nature, music, books, silence, passions, challenges, road trips, warm showers, the roofs over their heads.

When we slow down, take a deep breath, and are present, we see that we are filled with love and that an amazing world exists all around us.

To download this song for free,
please text Slowdown to the number 33444

~~~ Journal Questions ~~~

There can never be too much gratitude. Slow down and answer this question:

What are five offerings of gratitude you can make right now?

How might you offer that gratitude to yourself, nature, animals, another person, your god, or the universe? Pick one to five of these and write something about each for which you are grateful.

SHAKE IT

very time I sing this song, I feel connected to it. If I had to choose a favorite set of lyrics from this song, it would be the rap in the second verse:

> **We can make a difference**
> **There's different ways to deliver it**
> **Look inside and we will find**
> **The beauty that we're walking with**
> **Shed the snake skin, let the light in**
> **Here we go, c'mon now get ready to begin.**

As I have stated in many of the previous pages, we all have unique talents and strengths. This song is about combining those strengths and superpowers; it is about moving through the darkness of our journey into a place of light and hope. Even though it seems as if we are different from one another, we ultimately share more that is in common. We breathe, we eat, we sleep. We love, we get sad, we celebrate joy. We are born and we die. From what I can tell, we are also all in a search for meaning.

I open the first verse with lyrics that reflect what I just described:

I got a feeling
That you and me
We're looking for the same things
Searching for some meaning, about this life.

We experience a lot of uncertainty as we move through life, and it is important for us to discover what makes our lives worthwhile.

In the first verse I also say,

I got a feeling that you and me
We're just trying to work it out
We're trying to figure this life out
What living good is all about.

When I die I want to be able to say I lived a great life. I have had to work through a lot of challenges to gain perspective on what a good life might look like. I know it is different for you than it is for me, as it should be. The point is we are all searching, trying out new experiences to gain a deeper understanding of who we really are and what the good life means to us as individuals.

I have noticed that my *good life* concept changes as I engage in new experiences that either bring me closer to or push me further away from understanding how I might live the good life. There was a time in my life where that meant money; another time it was about my primary relationship. Recently, it is about helping the world to be a more peaceful and inspiring place to call home.

That is why I believe together we are the change that we can create in the world. That is what the chorus reveals:

Shake it with me, shake it with me, we are free
Shake it with me, shake it with me, we can believe
Shake it to the left, shake it to your right
Shake it through the darkness and step into your light.

Shake it with me, shake it with me, we can be
Shake it with me, we can be the change that we wanna see
Shake it to the left, shake it to your right
Shake it through the darkness and step into your light.

Shake it through the darkness--I personally experience darkness sometimes. I acknowledge it and choose to shake my way through it with the concepts you have already read about in this book. I *shake it* through by connecting to my dreams, my talents, and strengths. I *shake it* through by recognizing the power of gratitude. I *shake it* through by harnessing and creating amazing relationships with other like-minded people and learning from those who are dramatically different from me. I *shake it* through with patience and perspective by slowing down and making a plan.

My highest hope is that you are inspired to live an amazing life. I would love it if this song inspires you to grow stronger in your own personal contribution to the world. The lesson for me from writing this song is that we are stronger together than separate.

To download this song for free,
please text Shakeit to the number 33444

~~~ Journal Questions ~~~

Identify two or three people who inspire you. These could be people you know or don't know personally. Maybe they inspire you to show up stronger in your family, your work, your community, for yourself, or the world.

How might you spend a little more time with those people? Could you use the phone, video chat, buy their course, or meet them in person?

FLY AWAY

After I moved back to northern Michigan from Austin, Texas, I wanted to make brotha *James* a meaningful project that inspired people of all ages, kids included. I started to do what our small community calls family jams. One Sunday a month, five to ten families would get together and I would play a highly interactive concert. The parents would bring the toy drums, guitars, and any other instruments they could find for their kids to play.

Soon, a single mom named Jill started to show up at the monthly jams. She was a good bass player and her young son Ani was a cool ten-year old. After about four of these family jams I asked Jill out. She said yes and that was the beginning of the song "Fly Away."

To *fly away* means be present in the relationship and give it a fighting chance.

Relationships often fail because they are not made a priority. If you want to know if your relationship is a priority in your life, pull out your calendar and it will give you a snapshot. How often is a date night, a vacation, a family dinner out, a workout together, a walk in the woods, or carefree time set aside in your schedule? *Fly away* means put in equal effort to make the relationship work. I am going to try, will you try with me? Let us be a team.

The song starts with this verse:

> **First time we connected**
> **Sparked a little light**
> **When again we intersected**
> **I saw it as a sign.**
>
> **Based on my intentions**
> **And the passions in my life**
> **I'm ready for love's expression**
> **And what it is we're gonna find.**

I had been in relationships before but had never approached them with such curiosity and determination. In the past I was only really interested in what was in it for me, so this was a new experience. The second verse of the song is how I describe training myself to be a good partner:

> **Day by day I'm thinking about**
> **How to be your man**
> **Honesty and dreaming**
> **This is where I start my plans.**

Reciprocate your healing
I try to understand
What it is you're feeling
I think we can.

We know honesty is important and then having a vision for the future is also key in making a partnership strong. In the verse, I remind myself that I am thinking about her everyday--how to be her man, how to earn her love, how to make her proud to be with me.

The song's lyrics take me through a journey of how I want to show up in this relationship as well as all future ones. The chorus has three parts, and speaks to this purpose:

Fly away with me
Fly away with me

Fly ay ay ay ay away
Fly ay ay ay ay away

It's gonna be all right, fly away.

Relationships are work and you have to choose to *fly away* and make another person really important to make the relationship meaningful.

This also takes courage to commit deeply to someone else. It can be scary to put your heart on the line and take the risk of getting hurt. So the lyric "It's gonna be all right" is there to let both of us know that it is going to work out; we do not have to be afraid.

In these lyrics I am also telling her I will work hard and she is safe with me. That being said, sometimes I sing the lyrics and feel like a phony because I realize *Oops, I am doing a bad job right now of showing up*. I pay attention to what I observe in these moments and do my best to learn from them so I can live more of the lyrics everyday:

I open up my heart for you
I know you feel it too
That the time is right.

I will be more vulnerable, show up stronger, and be a better listener. I am also going to remember that my past does not equal my future. I can leave the memories of being cheated on and not loved behind in order to focus on the great things happening now. Sometimes our memories betray us with the stories they subtly whisper in our ear. Being aware that those stories exist is key. Acknowledge they are there, learn from them, and then let them dissolve. Easier said than done, I know.

When I started writing the song, I had no idea it would turn into the reggae rock song it is on the album. That was until Carlos and I were driving down Highway 71 on our way back from returning a rental car in Austin, Texas, and we heard a song on the radio; I commented *Wouldn't it be cool to make "Fly Away" have this type of feel?* Carlos agreed and for thirteen hours after arriving back at the studio we created what people will now experience as the produced version of the song.

Many lessons have emerged for me from working with this track. It is a commitment to be in a loving and flourishing relationship. Constant communication, patience, and being quiet are some of the skills I have gained. I have also come to understand much about putting another person's needs in front of my own. These past three years I have flown away with an amazing woman and I am really grateful for our adventure together. It is the best growing experience of my life.

To download this song for free,
please text Flyaway to the number 33444

 Journal Questions

What is the best time you have ever experienced in a relationship? (This could be a date, a trip, watching a movie, cuddling, talking, crying, etc.)

What is one awesome act you could do today for your partner?

If you don't have a partner, what is one nice action you could engage in today for someone you love or someone who loves you?

Turn off the TV
No more negativity
It's time to tune in
To a new frequency.
Say goodbye to news
That be giving you the blues
Turn that dial to the one that we can use.

Be careful about letting the media suck you in, specifically the craziness that is reality TV and the message of commercials; they are so good at making us think we want something we do not need. Both TV **and** social media can offer a newsfeed of controversy and negativity. I say turn off the source of the negativity; turn on the source that says we are all good enough. Tune into a frequency that makes us feel good about our lives and the amazing opportunities we have as human beings. It is up to us to decide what we watch and what we listen to.

Writing the pre-chorus of this song is one of the coolest creative moments I have shared with Carlos. The pre-chorus is all him, as well as the entire production of drums, bass, keys, fills:

The choice is mine
The choice is yours
Open up break down the doors.

The voice inside
Might be telling lies
I've had enough
Now I decide.

I love the way this sounds even when I say it to myself. Too many times I have been a victim of my own mind. Too often I reacted without really thinking; now, however, when my mind has a thought, I try to make more sense of it. I usually realize it is better not to say anything and just listen. If I did everything my mind told me to do, I might be in prison or dead.

Our minds literally have a mind of their own. At times we have to break down the doors and try new things, hang with new people, say no to actions or thoughts that drain us; this way we can become more aware of the voice that prevents us from being our best selves. The chorus reminds us

Whoa Whoa
I'm not my mind
Whoa Whoa
Now we decide.

We are not every thought that goes through our minds, so we should stop judging ourselves as if we were. It is time for us to decide who we want to be and what we want to stand for.

To download this song for free,
please text Notmymind to the number 33444

~~~ ## Journal Questions ~~~

When you pay attention to the chatter inside your head, what are the voices saying? Are they empowering voices or disempowering voices?

Can you track where these voices are coming from? TV, radio, movies, friends, family?

What is a new source of input you could start fueling yourself with? A podcast, positive music, more positive people?

If you were to have more positive input, how could you see that impacting the voices in your head?

And if those voices were more positive, what difference could that make in your life?

WARRIOR

Ever since I attended my first Tony Robbins event, I have been thinking about what it means to be a warrior in today's environment. What skills would a warrior possess? What type of work would he or she do? How would he or she act? How would we know if we saw a warrior? Am I a warrior?

When I think back to images of warriors in the past, I am instantly drawn to the Native Americans. Something about their inherent connection to nature has always stood out to me as noble and honorable. Of course, I also consider Tom Cruise in *The Last Samurai*, Kevin Costner in *Dances with Wolves*, Christian Bale in the *Dark Night*. And how about Dr. Martin Luther King Jr., Nelson Mandela, and our selfless soldiers? Warriors stand tall for their land, their people, their beliefs, themselves. They serve others, and that inspires me. I believe we all can be warriors.

The first verse of this song is about what I think we are made for:

Walk, talk, dance, sing
What is it that I'm meant to bring
My features, built for adventure
Loving one another is in my nature.

Hands, hair, eyes, skin
So much strength that's living within
My teacher, growing deeper,
Running with the land I am a leader.

I got the courage in me
Let go and let it release
Don't stop from feeling it,
It's time for me to break the stone.

I feel my fire inside
I'm growing up in this life
Into the human that I need to be
I know that I am not alone.

I see many warriors tackling the world's biggest challenges; by following their passions and taking risks, men like Elon Musk and women like Brene´ Brown are able to inspire entire movements to help the world evolve. Movies such as *What the Health*, *Cowspiracy* and *Before the Flood* are examples of art that challenges the status quo for our collective survival. How inspiring! Protecting Mother Earth is up to all of us as members of the collective society living on this planet. We might have to look at ourselves in the mirror and make some changes in order to be warriors. This thinking led me to create the bridge lyrics:

It's time to re-arrange
Turn the page
Entertain the notion
That we will find a way
Co-create
Let's step into these better days.

Now is the time for all of us to be warriors and to start asking what each of us can do to take ownership of our species' future. We live in uncertain times but we also have more access to information than ever before. We **will** find a way to overcome the many challenges, and we **will** create an amazing world to take care of the global community and our planet. We **can** do this. That is what the chorus proclaims:

I'm brave
I got what it takes
I am a warrior.
I'm brave
It's time to make a change
I am a warrior.

A warrior learns how to connect to his or her talents and strengths and then takes those strengths to the place that the world needs. Personally, I've noticed the intense need for patience and curiosity in connecting to my strengths and deeper personal meaning. In the second verse, I describe my connection to being curious about what is all around me, letting my pain pass through, and allowing for experiences that scare me to emerge.

Birds, bees, water, trees,
Curiosity in me
Attention
I'm ready for the question
Zone right in, get present with the lessons.

What does a warrior mean?
It means be brave
With how I treat
Connections
Put away the tension
I'm ready for the risk of a new direction.

Being brave means we need to confront our fears, and pain. When we allow ourselves to see our pain, we become more familiar with what it is and how it might be affecting us. As we move through this process, we see that the pain can be a magnificent teacher. And as we learn from the pain, we are able to gain an awareness of it and an ability not to be so affected by it. This helps us be more present, more useful, and more able to serve the world.

I see good things in me
I see the strengths I bring
No need to hesitate
It's time for me to make my move.

I let the pain pass through
Don't run, let in the truth
Sit down I'm gonna meditate
And put the pain into good use.

This track will always be one of my favorites to play; it so simply reminds me to step up and be a warrior for myself, my loved ones, and nature.

My highest hope for the song is that you consider all the ways you have been a warrior in your life as well as acknowledge the warriors you have connected with and have been inspired by.

To download this song for free,
please text Iamawarrior to the number 33444

~~~~ Journal Questions ~~~~

What does being a warrior mean to you?

For whom do you need to be a warrior? Yourself, your kids, your partner, your family, your friends, your colleagues, your clients?

When you look to the future, in what ways do you need to be a warrior to turn your dreams into reality?

ABRACADABRA

I am a musician
I make my music fun
I blast it on my run and when I need good energy.
I give it everything
It's in these words I sing
Fill 'em up with love, I paint these words and set them free.

I am a musical messenger on a mission to heal and inspire through the power of music. The words above are from the second verse of this song. My mission started as a passion I just loved to do, and it has turned into my purpose for being. I am doing my best to bring you great music that helps you feel alive. I also write these songs to give myself the love and motivation I need. This song is the best representation of what I'm doing as an inspirational musician.

The chorus helps me reflect on the importance of each word I use:

**With these words I create
Abracadabra
Laugh, are you ready to play
La la la la la
Let's make today a great day
With the words that we say.**

Both the words we listen to and the words we use play an enormous role in shaping our experience, with friends, money, success, physical appearance, and everything else we consider important.

Our words describe our world, when we talk to ourselves or when we talk to others. When we sing words that lift us up, we can be empowered. Words can inspire us to grow stronger and enable us to be more aware of who we are and what we must do in order to help one another thrive.

This song started with a conversation in the backyard of a Family Mastermind event at my good friend Mike McCarthy's house. At this event, twenty families had come together to talk about how to be well-rounded families.

On one particular evening, I started talking with Ian, a participant, and complimented him on his tattoos. After a short explanation about them, he said he was going to be getting a new one that said *abracadabra*. Then he asked me if I knew what *abracadabra* meant. I said ... magic? He chuckled and explained *abracadabra* means "with these words I create." Right away I was thinking those words would be an epic, meaningful song lyric with which I could have fun being creative.

What came to me as I worked on the song was that in so many ways I have created my brotha *James* journey based on the belief that "with these words I create." I am a big believer in affirmations. Throughout my adventure, I have confidently screamed, **"I am a musician."** (I probably have said it thousands of times at this point.) I have also talked about all the goals I possess for this mission with everyone that I know. When I heard what *abracadabra* meant, I knew it was symbolic of my journey, and I had to work it into a song. Little did I know that it would later become the title of the album. It is fitting though. So much of my mission and music is about the power of words.

Before I began writing this song I purchased a ukulele. As I learned to play, I started to hear the phrase "with these words I create" as a melody in the song. I started to imagine myself on stage with a uke in my hands, playing for ten thousand people, celebrating the idea that the words I use every single day create the lens through which I see the world. If I use negative words, it is inevitable that I will see more negativity in my everyday life. When I use positive words, I condition myself to see the world through a more affirming and opportunistic lens. I am so grateful to have a song that brings this thought process to life for myself and, of course, for the audience.

These lyrics affirm that our language patterns and word choices reflect the way we feel about our lives. Because of this song, I feel good every day. Even when I might be feeling a little low, I have found incredible ways to pull myself through with optimism and determination.

One of my favorite parts is the first verse:

I'm feeling good inside
I really love my life
I'm putting out these good vibes every single day.

I'm like a shining ray
I love to celebrate
Even on a rainy day I wear sunshine upon my face.

Each time I sing these opening lines, I smile and feel grateful. I am reminded of the light I want to be in the world. It only takes a couple seconds and the words energize me.

Through the process of writing this song, I realized how much work I still have to do with my own ability to use words to empower myself and others. The pre-chorus addresses the need to use our words as well as to reach out to others in our quest to be optimistic and positive:

Hello, my friend from another
Let go, and search for the good
I know, we got each other
It's so remarkably true
Whenever
I feel low
I look inside and grow
My words they help me know
Just who I am.

Think about how complex the world is and the skills we are given to navigate it. Our words are important tools to empower ourselves. You are in one of the most powerful networks on Earth--a network of positive, inspired people working to be the best they can be by doing good. My highest hope is that my music and my words help you realize this.

To download this song for free,
please text Abracadabra to the number 33444

~~~ Journal Questions ~~~

Think about the times you feel inspired and ready to make a dent in the universe. What are the words you could say to yourself that would compel you to reach your goal? This could be a short phrase or a long phrase; it could be a single word; it could be a story you are inspired by or anything else you can think of.

Words create worlds. What empowering words do you want to use to affirm the creation of your future?

CONCLUSION
AND ACKNOWLEDGEMENTS

T he journey to live my passion and celebrate inspirational music has just started. These stories behind the songs affirm my belief in the power of words (and music) to create a universe of community and love. We have the ability to shape our lives to find self-awareness, individual empowerment, fulfillment, and passion if we believe in ourselves and act on that belief. Be an animal! Be a warrior! Think Abracadabra and let your words create your universe.

To the Tribe--Before this book ends, I must offer sincere gratitude to the tribe that has believed in me and supported me. Whether you have been at a show, attended an empowerment conference, listened to my CD in your car, sat around a campfire and listened to me play, jammed with me in the basement of my house, or given me advice about what works (or doesn't work) in a song, I thank you for being on the journey with me. Your love, kindness, and trust are key to fulfilling my passion of writing music to uplift the world.

To Carlos--You are an amazing producer, musician, teacher, critic, and friend. Without you there would be no album. Being in your studio, working hard to be the best I can be, surrounded by the musicians you chose, gave me clarity of purpose for my work. Your passion has fed my passion. My appreciation does not end.

To Matt Duncan--Thank you for the support, the inspiration to write this book, and the artwork. Your work on the album and book is incredible.

To Family and Close Friends--Jamming at Christmas in the cul-de-sac, playing on the float for the crowds at Harbor Days, sitting in on a jam session in the living room, hammering out tunes at Driftwood, celebrating your wedding, affirming passion and purpose at an event--no matter where I have played music, I know that my community of family and close friends have encouraged, celebrated, listened to, and appreciated that music. You have had my back; you have made this journey fun. Your enthusiasm and encouragement allow me to believe in myself.

To Mom, Dad, and brother Sean--Without a doubt, there would be no brotha *James* without you. Your unconditional love has celebrated my successes and helped me understand the disappointments. Your faith in me has lifted my confidence in the most challenging times. Whether pounding pots and pans in the kitchen, experimenting with looping in the basement, strumming chords on the guitar around the kitchen table, or jamming with Sean at a festival, I knew your patience and belief in my dreams would always fuel my journey. Love has no limits as you three have shown me.

To Jill and Ani--It takes a lot to let a person you love travel around the world following his passion and purpose. I know it is not always easy and, at times, not what you want. Thank you for sharing me with the world. I will continue to grow as a human and musician. Simultaneously, I become a better man for the world when I am with you, and a better man for you when I am with the world. I love you two.

With deepest gratitude and love to all of you for
helping me make my dreams come true,

brotha *James*